Tennis Fe

(Advantages of playing Tennis and how to play Tennis)

Objective) "Simple is the best." Amateurs and hobbyists don't need an encyclopedia to play a sport for fun. It is the job of the umpire and service judge to lead professional matches. However, it is good to understand the basic rules. This book is to explain the advantages of playing Tennis and to show you how to play Tennis. You will have Tennis fever and love playing it.

COLLIN CHOI

DEDICATION

to racket sport players in the world..

CONTENTS

CHAP. 1. INTRODUCTION

"Tennis is a sport full of love because you will hear a lot of 'LOVES'."

Tennis is a racket sport which may be played individually against a single opponent (singles) or between two teams of two players each (doubles), using a tennis racket which is strung with cord to strike a rubber ball externally covered with felt over or around a net and into the opponent's court side. The objective of the game is to control and maneuver the ball in such a way that the opponent is not able to make a valid return. The player who fails to return the ball will not gain a point, on the contrary, the opposite player will do.

   Tennis is a part of Olympic games and is played at all levels of society and at all ages. The sport can be played by anyone who can hold a racket, including the challenged. The modern game of tennis originated in Birmingham, UK, in the late 19th century known as lawn tennis. During most of the 19th century, the term tennis referred to real tennis, not lawn tennis.

   The rules of modern tennis have changed a bit since the 1890s. Two exceptional cases are that from 1908 to 1961, the server had to keep one foot on the ground at all times, and the adoption of the tiebreak in the 1970s. A recent addition to professional tennis is the adoption of electronic review technology coupled with a point-challenge system, which allows a player to contest the line call of a point, a system also known as "Hawk-Eye."

Tennis is played by millions of recreational players and is a popular worldwide spectator sport, too. The four Grand Slam tournaments (also referred to as "the Majors") are especially popular

- the Australian Open: played on hard courts,
- the French Open: played on red clay courts,
- Wimbledon: played on grass courts, and
- the US Open: also played on hard courts.

TENNIS FEVER

CHAP. 2. ADVANTAGES

1) It can help you lose weight

One of the main benefits of playing Tennis is that it may help you lose weight. This is because it follows by a lot of movement that will lead to the breakdown of fat as well as helping to burn calories. Researchers discovered that if a man plays tennis for 1 hour he may burn up to 600 calories whereas a woman may burn up to 420 calories.

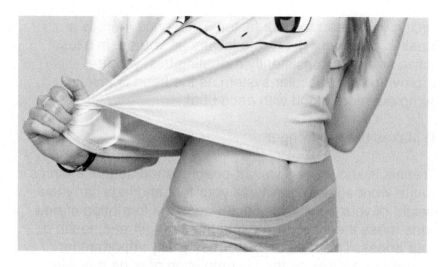

2) It is a head-to-toe workout

One of the main benefits of this sport is that your whole body gets an intensive workout. When you play a game, your legs are consistently in some form of motion whether that is running, jumping or bending. This leads to the muscles in your legs becoming stronger as they are continuously working hard to ensure you may play to the best of your ability.

Playing tennis involves using your top half a lot especially your shoulders and arms. When placing your body in the correct pose for a particular shot, the muscles in your upper half have to be strong enough to cope with twist's, turn's and swings so that you have control when hitting the ball.

3) It is good for your heart

As tennis is a sport which involves a lot of starting and stopping, your heart is trained to work in intervals. When you play a game, you are constantly moving around and forcing your heart to work faster. Then once there is a break in play, your heart rate lowers as you are in a less active state. By consistently repeating this, you are improving your vascular system as the heart is able to pump out more blood with each beat.

4) Makes bones stronger

Tennis is known as a weight-bearing sport so that it forces you to work against gravity as your feet and legs carry the weight of your body. This encourages the formation of new bone mass therefore increasing the strength and health of your bones. This type of exercise is vitally important for children and teens as the accumulation of bone mass in greater before and during puberty.

5) Improves your cognitive skills

Tennis requires a lot of thinking and decision making. You need to consider your body movements, the direction of the ball, your opponent's movements and even the conditions you are playing in from various angles. This way of thinking encourages you to quickly develop a strategy and execute it without over-analyzing it. By consistently making quick decisions which you then action, your cognitive skills will be improved both on and off the court as your brain will adopt this way of thinking when you are occasionally put under pressure.

6) Boosts your mood

Tennis, as with many other sports, releases a chemical called Endorphins produced by your central nervous system and pituitary gland. This chemical helps you to reduce stress levels and contributes to the "happy and pleasant feeling" which you get after doing something physical such as playing a sport. In addition, tennis is a great stress reliever. After a long hard day at the office or workplace, it is good to grab a racket and heading to a court to hit balls as this may allow you to get rid of your frustration and reduce your stress levels in a healthy and sound way.

7) It's a four-season sport

Tennis can be played all year round unlike many other sports. You may make use of indoor courts during the winter season and then when the hot weather arrives, you may go play outside in one of the many outdoor tennis courts. Superb for keeping active all year, tennis will help you keep New Year's resolutions and get that summer beach body with feeling happy.

8) Helps improve your social skills

Not only is tennis great for you physically but it can also have a positively mental influence. By joining a local tennis club or taking part in competitions, you can develop your social skills as you are interacting with other people. Additionally, it is an excellent and healthy way of catching up with friends and you can play either one on one or in doubles. The one thing to take a note about tennis is that sportsmanship is very important. In this sport, you may win as graciously as you may lose which is a valuable thing that can be applied to everyday life.

9) Develops and improves your work ethic

As with many other things in life, if you want to be good at something you need to work at it and the same can be said in Tennis. This is a sport which requires a lot of discipline, determination and most importantly passion. All of these will lead to a much stronger work ethic as you will be able to receive the rewards which can be achieved when you put your mind into something.

10) Anyone can play

The main beauty of Tennis is that anyone can play together. From the young to the old, this sport is played by generations due its strong sportsmanship value and fun nature. Regardless of your fitness level, skill level or age, Tennis can be played for fun as well competitively. Therefore, if you are looking for an interesting way to spend the afternoon or are struggling to find a way to keep the kids entertained during the holidays, then tennis will be a very good choice. Tennis really is a sport for everyone.

CHAP. 3. SIMPLE RULES

Before going over all different rules respectively for singles matches and doubles matches, we would review some of the general rules and regulations that apply to all of tennis before we learn how to play tennis for singles and doubles. The rules of tennis are slightly different for singles matches and doubles matches, although mostly similar.

3.1. General Rules of Tennis

i.   A ball must land within bounds for play to continue; if a player hits the ball outside of bounds, this results in the loss of the point for them.

ii.   Players/teams cannot touch the net or posts or cross onto the opponent's side.

iii. Players/teams cannot carry the ball or catch it with the racquet.

iv. Players cannot hit the ball twice.

v. Players must wait until the ball passes the net before they can return it.

vi. A player that does not return a live ball before it bounces twice loses the point.

vii. If the ball hits or touches the players, that counts as a penalty.

viii. If the racquet leaves the hand or verbal abuse occurs, a penalty is given.

ix. Any ball that bounces on the lines of boundary are considered good.

x. A serve must bounce first before the receiving player can return it.

3.2. Equipment

1) Racquet – A racquet is comprised of a handle, a frame, and strings that are bound in a crisscross weaving pattern. A racquet's frame should not exceed 32 inches in length, with a handle no longer than 12.5 inches in width, and a surface no more than 15.5 inches in overall length or 11.5 inches in width. There can also be no objects or devices on the racquet except for ones that prevent vibration and wear

and tear.

2) Ball – A tennis ball is white or yellow in color for tournaments, with measurements of 2-1/2 to 2-5/8 inches in diameter and weighing anywhere from 2 to 2-1/16 ounces. The elasticity of the ball and the uniform outer surface are also determined by approved specifications.

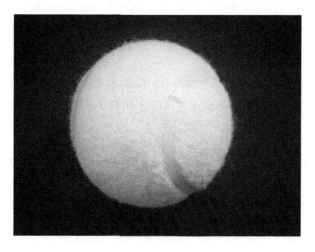

3.3. Scoring

i.   Points – Smallest unit of measurement. Points increment from Love(0)-15-30-40-game.

ii.   Games – Games consist of 4 points each, and is won when a player reaches 4 points with at least a 2 point advantage.

iii.   Sets – A set consists of 6 games and is won by the player/team who reaches 6 games first with least a 2 point lead.

iv.   Advantage Set – If a game score of 6-6 is reached and advantage set rules are used, a player/team can only win a set with a 2 game lead.

v.   Matches – A match is usually played as best of 3 or

best of 5 sets.

vi. Deuce – Occurs if a score of 40-40 is reached. In order to win the game, a player/team must win 2 consecutive points in order to take the game. If a player wins one point, they have advantage, but if they lose the next point, the score returns to deuce.

vii. Tie-break game – If a game score of 6-6 is reached and tie-break set rules are used, players must play a tie-break game in order to decide who wins the set. In a tie-break game, a player/team must reach 7 points with a two point advantage to win. For the serving format of a tie-break game, player 1 serves for the first point, player 2 serves for the next two points, player 1 serves for the next two points after that, etc.

3.4. Tennis court measurements

Official measurements of a typical tennis court are as follows.

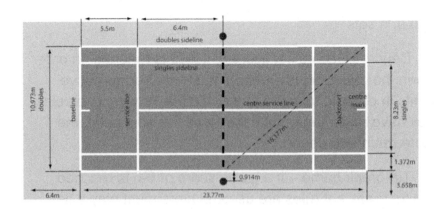

(In meters)

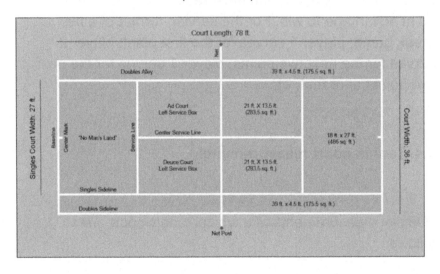

(in feet)

i.   Baseline – The baselines are the lines on either end of the court that determines the boundaries of play going lengthwise. They are also where a player serves behind.

ii.   Center Mark – The center mark determines the two

halves of the tennis court. It mainly helps with service to determine where a player should stand prior to serving.

iii.   Center Line – The center line divides the two service boxes into a distinct left service box and right service box on either side of the court. Landing a serve on the line is considered good.

iv.   Net – The net stands 3 feet and 6 inches high where the posts lie while the middle of the net is 3 feet tall, with the posts 3 feet outside of the court on either side. Hitting a ball into the net is considered an out while any ball that hits the net cord and falls onto the other side is considered good except for a serve, which allows for a re-do, or let.

v.   Service Line – The service line separates the forecourt from the back court, and it also marks the length of the service box.

vi.   Singles Sideline – The singles sideline is the innermost line running lengthwise and determines the boundary of play for singles matches as well as the width of the service box.

vii.   Doubles Sideline – The doubles sideline is the outermost line running lengthwise and is only used in doubles matches.

3.5. Who Serves First?

A flip of the coin or spin of the racket, known as the toss, determines which player or team serves first. If called correctly, the player or team that did so chooses who serves first. The player/team who did not call it correctly decides which side of the court they want to play on first.

3.6. Rally

The rally consists of the exchange of shots after the serve is made until a player/team makes a mistake and loses the point. Any shot that is hit within bounds is considered good and allows the rally to continue. If you want to learn how to play tennis, you will need to know how to rally consistently.

3.7. Serving and Choosing Sides

Foot Fault – A foot fault is when a player steps into the court or crosses the center mark before they have made contact with the ball. This results in the loss of the serve.

Proper Serve – A player serves on the right side of the court at the beginning of each game, with the goal of serving the ball into the diagonal service box. If the serve lands in the correct service box, play can continue. The server switches to serve on the left side for the next point, and vice versa until the game is over.

1) How to serve correctly

Players serve from the right side of the court at the beginning of each game, trying to land their shot into the opposite side's diagonal service box

(Diagonally)

2) First Service: The server is allowed two chances to land their ball into the service box. The first attempt is known as the first service. Failing the first service leads to the second service.

3) Second Service: The second attempt is known as the second service. Failing the second service results in the loss of the point.

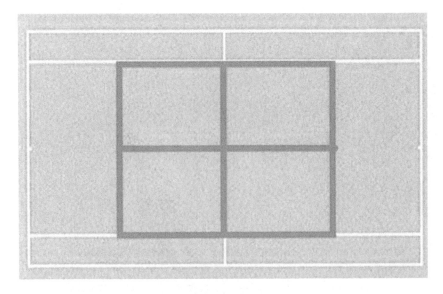

(Service box)

4) Let: A let is a re-do given to a player who serves although the ball hits the net cord before falling into the correct service box. You are allowed an infinite amount of lets, although it does not happen often.

5) Order of Service: The player/team who wins the toss serves first (team that wins chooses which player serves). If playing singles matches, players alternate between serving and receiving every game. If playing doubles matches, teams alternate between serving and receiving every game, with each player on a team getting the chance to serve before the cycle repeats.

Positions on the Court
Singles
i) during the service ii) after the service

Legend: *A - server*
        B - receiver

Doubles
i) during the service ii) after the service

Legend: *A - server   C - receiver*
        B - server's partner   D - receiver's partner

6) Switching Sides – Players/teams switch sides for every odd-numbered game (so, games 3, 5, 7 etc.)

3.8. Singles Vs. Doubles Tennis Rules

The tennis rules for singles and doubles matches are a little different, although mainly regarding serving order and court size. Doubles tennis rules are just slightly adapted to make room for an extra player on either side of the court, but for the most part, doubles tennis rules are very much the same as singles matches. So, here's how to play tennis for singles and doubles matches.

3.8.1. Singles Tennis Rules

1) Court Size

A singles court uses the innermost sideline and measures a total of 27 feet(8.23 meter) wide by 78 feet(23.77 meter) long.

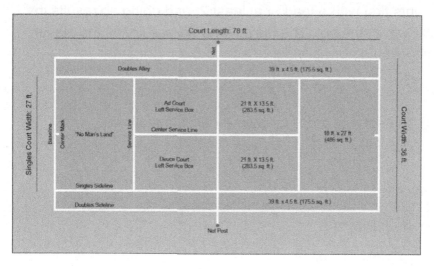

2) Serving Order

The player who wins the toss chooses who serves first. Whomever is serving first serves for the entire duration of the first game. After the game, the next server will be the player who received last, serving for the duration of the second game. For every odd-numbered game, players switch sides of the court.

3) Tie-Break Serving Order

If a score of 6-6 is reached and tie-break rules are used, a tie-break game is played in order to determine which player wins the set. For a tie-break game, the goal is to reach 7 points first with a lead of at least 2, and doing so results in the win of the set. The player who serves first is the player who would normally serve after 6-6, or 12 games.

4) The serving order for a tie-break is as follows:

Point 1: Player A

Point 2: Player B

Point 3: Player B

Point 4: Player A

Point 5: Player A

Point 6: Player B

Point 7: Player B

Point 8: Player A

Point 9: Player A

...

5) Match Format

A singles match is often played to the best of 3 sets, although some men's singles tournaments play to the best of 5. It really all depends on the preferences of the players on the rules of the tournament.

3.8.2. Doubles Tennis Rules

1) Court Size

A doubles court uses the outermost sideline and measures a total of 36 feet(10.97 meter) wide by 78 feet(23.77 meter) long.

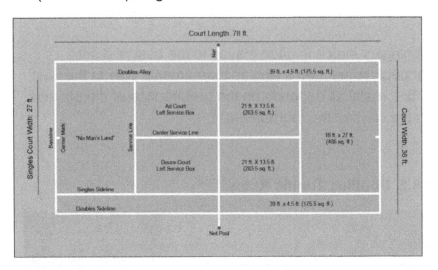

2) Serving Order

The team who wins the toss chooses which team serves first, and that team will choose which of them will serve first. Whoever is serving first serves for the entire duration of the first game. After the game, the next server will be chosen by that team and will serve for the duration of the second game. For every odd-numbered game, teams switch sides of the court, and the player who hasn't served yet from the first game must now serve, and the player who hasn't served yet from the second team serves afterward, and so on.

3) Tie-Break Serving Order

The serving order for a tie-break is as follows:

Point 1: Player A

Point 2: Player X

Point 3: Player X

Point 4: Player B

Point 5: Player B

Point 6: Player Y

Point 7: Player Y

Point 8: Player A

Point 9: Player A

…

4) Match Format

A doubles match is often played to the best of 5 sets.

COLLIN CHOI

CHAP. 5. TENNIS SKILLS AND TECHNIQUES

Tennis skills and techniques are related to the technical, physical and mental skills and abilities of a player. These fundamental tennis skills and techniques are necessary for players to reach an high tennis level and are also essential in the development of a tennis player's game.

A diversified set of tennis skills and techniques is required if a tennis player desires to make progress in tennis. Players must possess a wide range of different tennis skills and techniques including stroke production, strategy, mental toughness, and physical athleticism.

5.1. Fundamental Tennis Skills and Techniques

The fundamental tennis technical skills that every beginner player should acquire are explained as below. Additional skills may be acquired as players mature and become more knowledgeable of the more advanced technical skills. Some examples of these advanced skills are

- net play
- net charge
- making contact
- slice
- drop shots
- swing and many others.

Only the fundamental tennis skills and techniques are described here.

5.1.1. Forehand

The forehand stroke is considered as the most natural stroke in tennis. The forehand stroke takes the number one part of tennis skills and techniques for most players from beginner to professional tennis players.

If you are a right-handed player, and your opponent returns a ball directly towards your body, your tendency is to step to your left and hit the ball from the right side of your body. If you are a left-handed player, and your opponent returns a point directly towards your body, you naturally step to your right and hit the ball from the left side of your body.

Because the forehand stroke is a type of a natural stroke, this stroke is performed more frequently by players in tennis matches compared to any other tennis strokes.

5.1.2. Backhand

The backhand stroke is made from the opposite side of your forehand stroke. Thus, if you are a right-handed player, you hit the ball from the left side of your body. If you are a left-handed player, you hit the ball from the right side of your body.

To correctly make the efficient backhand stroke, you must bring back you dominant hand or racket hand around your body before you hit the ball.

The backhand stroke can be unnatural to make at the beginning. But if you familiarize and practice it regularly, it can be a very good additional stroke to your tennis skills and techniques.

5.1.3. Serve

The serve is the beginning of a point in a tennis game. The player who serves is called the "Server" and the player on the other end is called the "Receiver." There are several types of serves such as topspin, topspin-slice, flat, slice, kick and many others. Since the serve begins every point, it is very important to develop this skill among other tennis skills and techniques.

A perfect serve is achieved by taking the right stance, the right serve grip and the correct ball toss. Additionally, power can also be added if the server already has the ability to create the proper body movements such as knee bending and body coiling, the right racket swing and the right point of contact. Most importantly, the serve must be developed as a primary attack weapon while achieving pinpoint precision and depth.

5.1.4. Overhead

A overhead is a shot hit above the player's head like the serve shot. It is also called as a smash shot because it is usually hit with the power. If made correctly, it gives a point to the smasher. While a lob shot is normally hit down deep, an overhead shot is normally hit near the net or in the middle of the court. In some cases, a poorly executed lob shot, not very high and not to deep, may be returned as an overhead shot by the opponent player. To add more power to an overhead shot, you may hit it before it bounces on the ground.

5.1.5. Volley

A volley is a shot where the ball is hit before it bounces on the ground except for the overhead shot and the serve. In most cases, a volley is hit when you are playing near the net. Nevertheless, it can also be hit even if you are in the middle or even on the baseline depending on the playing circumstances.

A volley is considered as a part of the overall tennis skills and techniques that can be applied properly when you are off balance or out-of-position to hit a groundstroke. However, it is normally played as an offensive shot near the net, where you hit a winner angled or a well placed volley shot.

5.1.6. Lob

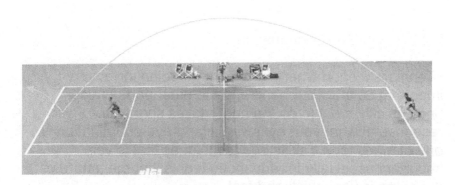

A lob shot is an additionally important one to add to a player's tennis skills and techniques. It is a shot that can be used as either an offensive or defensive shot. A lob shot is made by hitting the ball high and deep into your opponent's court. Normally, an offensive lob shot is hit when the opponent is standing at the net. Whilst the defensive lob shot is used to force the opponent back and allow you to recover your better defensive position. As a result, you can gain back the control of the play and make it to your advantage. A lob shot is another addition to the player's tennis skills and techniques that ensures a point.

5.2. Physical requirements

5.2.1. General athletic ability

The game of tennis involves a lot of physical activities. It requires speed, agility, flexibility, and endurance that any players to want to reach the elite level must have. These are among tennis skills and techniques needed to be a good player. You need speed to run for a ball as quickly as possible and you need agility and alertness to anticipate your opponent's shot. Your muscles and tendons need to be flexible for you to be able to hit a ball that may seem unreachable. Lastly, you need to have the endurance and stamina to last long hours of tennis matches.

5.2.2. Hand-Eye-Coordination

Tennis is a sport where hand-eye coordination is very important so that your hand and the other parts of your body quickly react to do the right moves shortly in response of what your eyes see. Hand-eye-coordination is one of many tennis skills and techniques that is very important especially for advanced tennis that the nature of the game is very quick and fast.

5.2.3. Balance

Balance is one of the very important physical tennis skills and techniques a player must have. Balance is crucial to hit well placed and accurate shots. Good balance also minimizes injuries especially in the lower part of your body such as the legs, ankles and knees. Exercises and drills to improve balance can be done both on court and off-court.

5.3. Mental requirements

5.3.1. Motivation

Without motivation, tennis skills and techniques are of few use. Like other businesses, having the motivation to accomplish something is the source of many successful individuals in their own fields. The same is applied to tennis players. Beginners have to have motivation to learn the different tennis skills and tactics for them to improve and succeed. Professional players on one hand, must be motivated enough to be victors.

5.3.2. Concentration and focus

Concentration and focus play a vital role in every tennis player's performance. To keep concentrating while you are on court means you have to remove all the other thoughts especially the negative ones that can distract you in mind. Concentration is required to let your first serve in especially during crucial points or you should focus not to miss your second serve to avoid double faults. Concentration is not only important on court but off court as well such as during practice. You need to try to have a full concentration for you to improve your tennis skills and techniques during regular practice.

5.3.3. Competitive spirit

Tennis is a tough match particularly for tennis singles. It can become tougher if the match is not going your way because you stand alone out there on court. Your competitive spirit is tested while you are racing against the leading opponent. The way you manage the situation when you are losing will be determined on your competitive ability. A competitive player does not give up until the game is announced over.

5.3.4. Problem-solving

In tennis, a player must voluntarily set up a game plan and tactics in advance whoever the opponent will be. However, a game plan does not work well all the time. The player has to find ways to stop the opponent's momentum for her or her not to be out played. The player needs to come up with his or her own solutions in case the tactics are not much effective on court.

CHAP. 6. KEYS OF TENNIS TECHNIQUES

1. Tennis Grips

Tennis stroke production and overall tennis techniques closely relate to tennis grips. As the game of tennis has evolved, the grips have changed accordingly. For example, on the forehand, players are now using semi-western grips rather than the old eastern and continental grips. There are several inherent advantages to these slightly more extreme grips. When you combine modern tennis techniques with a grip closer to semi-western, you will notice that you can swing harder with less effort and still keep the ball in play.

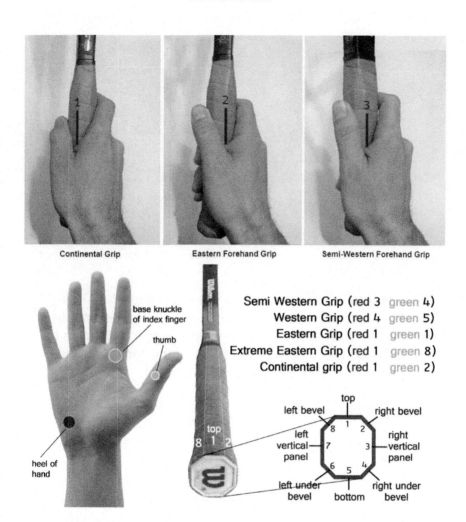

Continental Grip   Eastern Forehand Grip   Semi-Western Forehand Grip

base knuckle
of index finger

thumb

heel of
hand

Semi Western Grip (red 3 green 4)
Western Grip (red 4 green 5)
Eastern Grip (red 1 green 1)
Extreme Eastern Grip (red 1 green 8)
Continental grip (red 1 green 2)

top

left bevel   right bevel

top   left   right
8 1 2   vertical   vertical
           panel   panel

left under   right under
bevel   bottom   bevel

2. Unit Turn

The unit turn in tennis is one of the most important key aspects of tennis technique. Simply speaking, the unit turn is where the body and racket turn sideways together as a "unit" to begin the preparation phase of the tennis stroke, whether its forehand or backhand strokes.

3. Swing Shape

The swing shape is how you position the racket and arm through the course of the take-back. Most beginner level players make the mistake of having excess motion in their take-back, and others have various flaws throughout the take-back which limit their ability to generate power and spin.

4. Lowering and "Drop"

This is probably the least trained and the most significant. If you study the strokes of professional players, you will recognize that as 'the racket' head falls, it drops inside towards their legs first. This positions the racket head to facilitate optimum efficiency.

5. Kinetic Chain

The kinetic chain is a scientific term used in tennis technique to describe the linking and unlinking of the body parts. High level of players synchronize their body to flow with their strokes, utilizing every inch of rotation and time the ball perfectly to their contact.

CHAP. 7. ORGANIZATION AND TOURNAMENTS

• Type: Outdoor or indoor
• First played: between 1859 and 1865, Birmingham, England
• Equipment: Tennis ball, tennis racket, net, shoes and etc.
• Team members: Singles or doubles
• Mixed gender: Separate tours & mixed doubles
• Olympic:
    - Summer Olympic program since 1988
    - Summer Paralympics' program since 1992
• Highest governing body
:   ITF (International Tennis Federation)
• Grand Slam Tournaments:

Tournament	Location	Surface	Date
Australian Open	Melbourne	Hard (Plexicushion)	January–February
French Open	Paris	Clay	May–June
Wimbledon	London	Grass	June–July
US Open	New York City	Hard (DecoTurf)	August–September

TENNIS FEVER

CHAP. 8. ETIQUETTE

Of all sports, tennis is famous for its etiquette. Tennis etiquette actually makes the sport more pleasant and enjoyable, while explaining a dozen of rules about how to behave on a tennis court may sound old-fashioned. Good tennis etiquette won't give you a better serve or a more accurate backhand shot but it will give you more fun to share a court with.

1) Wait your turn
When your turn comes, let the people before you to finish the game they are playing before taking over the court. Don't barge your way onto court until your allotted booking time. Flexing your biceps courtside won't enhance your predecessors' concentration and might earn you some tennis balls.

2) Warm-up
Keep your pre-match warm-up brief. Professional players stick to five minutes, and so better you.

3) Toss a coin
To decide who will serve first, toss a coin or spin a racquet. The person who wins the toss may choose to serve, receive, pick which end of the court they would like or even make their opponent choose.

4) Got two balls?
Make sure the server always has two balls at their end of the court. When you are feeding balls up the court, hit or roll them gently within reach of the server, you don't delay play by spraying them around.

5) Serve the right way
Before you serve, you make sure your opponent is ready to receive. While the rules say you should take no more than 20 seconds between points, you don't want to win a point by serving at your opponent's back.

6) No return necessary

If your opponent serves a first-serve fault, you don't hit a return back unless the call was so close that you had no option but to hit the ball.

7) Walk with care
Don't walk behind another court during a point, across someone else's court while they are in the middle of a game or interrupt a point on another court to retrieve a ball.

8) In or out?
While it's rude to question your opponent's line calls, if you really think you are being diddled ask once, firmly: "are you sure?" then move on.

9) Scoring made easy
If you are serving, you call the score out loudly and clearly. It will help to minimize disagreements.

10) Respect
Be respectful of your opponent. While it is fine to celebrate your successes, it is not polite to pump your fists, hiss "yes" or high-five spectators when your opponent makes an error.

11) Lucky!
Apologize if you win a lucky point or if you accidentally hit your opponent with a ball.

12) Concentrate on your match
Keep your attention on the court. You don't chat with spectators, interrupt a game to answer your mobile phone, file your nails at the change of ends or do anything else that might distract your opponent or delay play.

13) We are adults
Don't have a tantrum if things are not going your way. You behave like an adult without frowning.

14) Congratulations
Shake hands firmly and congratulate your opponent at the end of the match..

COLLIN CHOI

APPENDIX. Ⅰ. OFFICIAL RULES

The international rules are governed by ITF (International Tennis Federation). This article also can be found at https://www.itftennis.com/technical/publications/rules/overvi ew.aspx.

1. THE COURT

The court shall be a rectangle, 78 feet (23.77 m) long and, for singles matches, 27 feet (8.23 m) wide. For doubles matches, the court shall be 36 feet (10.97 m) wide.

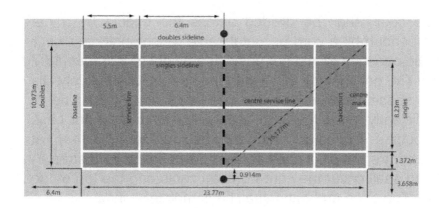

(In meters)

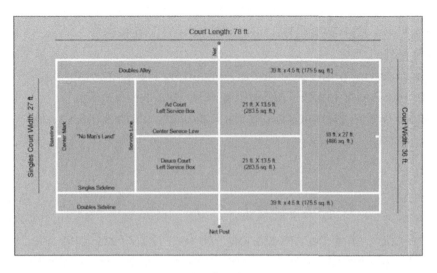

(in feet)

The court shall be divided across the middle by a net suspended by a cord or metal cable which shall pass over or be attached to two net posts at a height of 3 ½ feet (1.07 m). The net shall be fully extended so that it completely fills the space between the two net posts and it must be of sufficiently small mesh to ensure that a ball cannot pass through it. The height of the net shall be 3 feet (0.914 m) at the centre, where it shall be held down tightly by a strap. A band shall cover the cord or metal cable and the top of the net. The strap and band shall be completely white.

• The maximum diameter of the cord or metal cable shall be 1/3 inch (0.8 cm).

• The maximum width of the strap shall be 2 inches (5 cm).

• The band shall be between 2 inches (5 cm) and 2 ½ inches (6.35 cm) deep on each side.

For doubles matches, the centres of the net posts shall be 3 feet (0.914 m) outside the doubles court on each side.

For singles matches, if a singles net is used, the centres of the net posts shall be 3 feet (0.914 m) outside the singles court on each side. If a doubles net is used, then the net shall be supported, at a height of 3 ½ feet (1.07 m), by two singles sticks, the centres of which shall be 3 feet (0.914 m) outside the singles court on each side.

• The net posts shall not be more than 6 inches (15 cm) square or 6 inches (15 cm) in diameter.

• The singles sticks shall not be more than 3 inches (7.5 cm) square or 3 inches (7.5 cm) in diameter.

• The net posts and singles sticks shall not be more than 1 inch (2.5 cm) above the top of the net cord.

The lines at the ends of the court are called baselines and the lines at the sides of the court are called sidelines.

Two lines shall be drawn between the singles sidelines, 21 feet (6.40 m) from each side of the net, parallel with the net. These lines are called the servicelines. On each side of the net, the area between the serviceline and the net shall be divided into two equal parts, the service courts, by the centre serviceline. The centre serviceline shall be drawn parallel with the singles sidelines and half way between them.

Each baseline shall be divided in half by a centre mark, 4 inches (10 cm) in length, which shall be drawn inside the court and parallel with the singles sidelines.

• The centre service line and centre mark shall be 2 inches (5 cm) wide.

• The other lines of the court shall be between 1 inch (2.5 cm) and 2 inches (5 cm) wide, except that the baselines may be up to 4 inches (10 cm) wide.

All court measurements shall be made to the outside of the lines and all lines of the court shall be of the same colour clearly contrasting with the colour of the surface.

No advertising is allowed on the court, net, strap, band, net posts or singles sticks except as provided in Appendix IV.

In addition to the court described above, the court designated as "Red" and the court designated as "Orange" in Appendix VII can be used for 10 and under tennis competition.

Note: Guidelines for minimum distances between the baseline and backstops and between the sidelines and side-stops can be found in Appendix IX.

2. PERMANENT FIXTURES

The permanent fixtures of the court include the backstops and side-stops, the spectators, the stands and seats for spectators, all other fixtures around and above the court, the chair umpire, line umpires, net umpire and ball persons when in their recognised positions.

In a singles match played with a doubles net and singles sticks, the net posts and the part of the net outside the singles sticks are permanent fixtures and are not considered as net posts or part of the net.

3. THE BALL

Balls, which are approved for play under the Rules of Tennis, must comply with the specifications in Appendix I.

The International Tennis Federation shall rule on the question of whether any ball or prototype complies with Appendix I or is otherwise approved, or not approved, for play. Such ruling may be taken on its own initiative or upon application by any party with a bona fide interest therein, including any player, equipment manufacturer or National Association or members thereof. Such rulings and applications shall be made in accordance with the applicable Review and Hearing Procedures of the International Tennis Federation (see Appendix XI).

The event organisers must announce in advance of the event:

a.   The number of balls for play (2, 3, 4 or 6).

b.   The ball change policy, if any.

Ball changes, if any, can be made either:

i.   After an agreed odd number of games, in which case, the first ball change in the match shall take place two games earlier than for the rest of the match, to make allowance for the warm-up. A tie-break game counts as one game for the ball change. A ball change shall not take place at the beginning of a tie-break game. In this case, the ball change shall be delayed until the beginning of the second game of the next set; or

ii.   At the beginning of a set

If a ball gets broken during play, the point shall be replayed.

Case 1: If a ball is soft at the end of a point, should the point be replayed?

Decision: If the ball is soft, not broken, the point shall not be replayed.

Note: Any ball to be used in a tournament which is played under the Rules of Tennis must be named on the official ITF list of approved balls issued by the International Tennis Federation.

4. THE RACKET

Rackets, which are approved for play under the Rules of Tennis, must comply with the specifications in Appendix II.

The International Tennis Federation shall rule on the question of whether any racket or prototype complies with Appendix II or is otherwise approved, or not approved, for play. Such ruling may be undertaken on its own initiative or upon application by any party with a bona fide interest therein, including any player, equipment manufacturer or National Association or members thereof. Such rulings and applications shall be made in accordance with the applicable Review and Hearing Procedures of the International Tennis Federation (see Appendix XI).

Case 1: Is more than one set of strings allowed on the hitting surface of a racket? Decision: No. The rule mentions a pattern (not patterns) of crossed strings. (See Appendix II)

Case 2: Is the stringing pattern of a racket considered to be generally uniform and flat if the strings are on more than one plane? Decision: No.

Case 3: Can vibration damping devices be placed on the strings of a racket? If so, where can they be placed?

Decision: Yes, but these devices may only be placed outside the pattern of the crossed strings.

Case 4: During a point, a player accidentally breaks the strings. Can the player continue to play another point with this racket?

Decision: Yes, except where specifically prohibited by event organisers.

Case 5: Is a player allowed to use more than one racket at any time during play?

Decision: No.

Case 6: Can a battery that affects playing characteristics be incorporated into a racket?

Decision: No. A battery is prohibited because it is an energy source, as are solar cells and other similar devices.

5. SCORE IN A GAME

a. Standard game

A standard game is scored as follows with the server's score being called first:

No point	-	"Love"
First point	-	"15"
Second point	-	"30"
Third point	-	"40"
Fourth point	-	"Game"

except that if each player/team has won three points, the score is "Deuce". After "Deuce", the score is "Advantage" for the player/team who wins the next point. If that same player/team also wins the next point, that player/team wins the "Game"; if the opposing player/team wins the next point, the score is again "Deuce". A player/team needs to win two consecutive points immediately after "Deuce" to win the "Game".

b.   Tie-break game

During a tie-break game, points are scored "Zero", "1", "2", "3", etc. The first player/team to win seven points wins the "Game" and "Set", provided there is a margin of two points over the opponent(s). If necessary, the tie-break game shall continue until this margin is achieved.

The player whose turn it is to serve shall serve the first point of the tie-break game. The following two points shall be served by the opponent(s) (in doubles, the player of the opposing team due to serve next). After this, each player/team shall serve alternately for two consecutive points until the end of the tie-break game (in doubles, the rotation of service within each team shall continue in the same order as during that set).

The player/team whose turn it was to serve first in the tie-break game shall be the receiver in the first game of the following set.

Additional approved alternative scoring methods can be found in Appendix V.

6.   **SCORE IN A SET**

There are different methods of scoring in a set. The two main methods are the "Advantage Set" and the "Tie-break Set". Either method may be used provided that the one to be used is announced in advance of the event. If the "Tie-break Set" method is to be used, it must also be announced whether the final set will be played as a "Tie-break Set" or an "Advantage Set".

a.   "Advantage Set"

The first player/team to win six games wins that "Set", provided there is a margin of two games over the opponent(s). If necessary, the set shall continue until this margin is achieved.

b.   "Tie-break Set"

The first player/team to win six games wins that "Set", provided there is a margin of two games over the opponent(s). If the score reaches six games all, a tie-break game shall be played.

Additional approved alternative scoring methods can be found in Appendix V.

7.   SCORE IN A MATCH

A match can be played to the best of 3 sets (a player/team needs to win 2 sets to win the match) or to the best of 5 sets (a player/team needs to win 3 sets to win the match).

Additional approved alternative scoring methods can be found in Appendix V.

8. SERVER & RECEIVER

The players/teams shall stand on opposite sides of the net. The server is the player who puts the ball into play for the first point. The receiver is the player who is ready to return the ball served by the server.

Case 1: Is the receiver allowed to stand outside the lines of the court?

Decision: Yes. The receiver may take any position inside or outside the lines on the receiver's side of the net.

9. CHOICE OF ENDS & SERVICE

The choice of ends and the choice to be server or receiver in the first game shall be decided by toss before the warm-up starts. The player/team who wins the toss may choose:

a.   To be server or receiver in the first game of the match, in which case the opponent(s) shall choose the end of the court for the first game of the match; or

b.   The end of the court for the first game of the match, in which case the opponent(s) shall choose to be server or receiver for the first game of the match; or

c.   To require the opponent(s) to make one of the above choices.

Case 1: Do both players/teams have the right to new choices if the warm-up is stopped and the players leave the court?

Decision: Yes. The result of the original toss stands, but new choices may be made by both players/teams.

10. CHANGE OF ENDS

The players shall change ends at the end of the first, third and every subsequent odd game of each set. The players shall also change ends at the end of each set unless the total number of games in that set is even, in which case the players change ends at the end of the first game of the next set.

During a tie-break game, players shall change ends after every six points.

Additional approved alternative procedures can be found in Appendix V.

11. BALL IN PLAY

Unless a fault or a let is called, the ball is in play from the moment the server hits the ball, and remains in play until the point is decided.

12. BALL TOUCHES A LINE

If a ball touches a line, it is regarded as touching the court bounded by that line.

13. BALL TOUCHES A PERMANENT FIXTURE

If the ball in play touches a permanent fixture after it has hit the correct court, the player who hit the ball wins the point. If the ball in play touches a permanent fixture before it hits the ground, the player who hit the ball loses the point.

14. ORDER OF SERVICE

At the end of each standard game, the receiver shall become the server and the server shall become the receiver for the next game.

In doubles, the team due to serve in the first game of each set shall decide which player shall serve for that game. Similarly, before the second game starts, their opponents shall decide which player shall serve for that game. The partner of the player who served in the first game shall serve in the third game and the partner of the player who served in the second game shall serve in the fourth game. This rotation shall continue until the end of the set.

15. ORDER OF RECEIVING IN DOUBLES

The team which is due to receive in the first game of a set shall decide which player shall receive the first point in the game. Similarly, before the second game starts, their opponents shall decide which player shall receive the first point of that game. The player who was the receiver's partner for the first point of the game shall receive the second point and this rotation shall continue until the end of the game and the set. After the receiver has returned the ball, either player in a team can hit the ball.

Case 1: Is one member of a doubles team allowed to play alone against the

opponents?

Decision: No.

16. THE SERVICE

Immediately before starting the service motion, the server shall stand at rest with both feet behind (i.e. further from the net than) the baseline and within the imaginary extensions of the centre mark and the sideline.

The server shall then release the ball by hand in any direction and hit the ball with the racket before the ball hits the ground. The service motion is completed at the moment that the player's racket hits or misses the ball. A player who is able to use only one arm may use the racket for the release of the ball.

17. SERVING

When serving in a standard game, the server shall stand behind alternate halves of the court, starting from the right half of the court in every game.

In a tie-break game, the service shall be served from behind alternate halves of the court, with the first served from the right half of the court.

The service shall pass over the net and hit the service court diagonally opposite, before the receiver returns it.

18. FOOT FAULT

During the service motion, the server shall not:

a.   Change position by walking or running, although slight movements of the feet are permitted; or

b.   Touch the baseline or the court with either foot; or

c. Touch the area outside the imaginary extension of the sideline with either foot; or

d. Touch the imaginary extension of the centre mark with either foot.

If the server breaks this rule it is a "Foot Fault".

Case 1: In a singles match, is the server allowed to serve standing behind the part of the baseline between the singles sideline and the doubles sideline? Decision: No.

Case 2: Is the server allowed to have one or both feet off the ground?

Decision: Yes.

19. SERVICE FAULT

The service is a fault if:

a. The server breaks Rules 16, 17 or 18; or

b.   The server misses the ball when trying to hit it; or

c.   The ball served touches a permanent fixture, singles stick or net post before it hits the ground; or

d.   The ball served touches the server or server's partner, or anything the server or server's partner is wearing or carrying.

Case 1: After tossing a ball to serve, the server decides not to hit it and catches it instead. Is this a fault?

Decision: No. A player, who tosses the ball and then decides not to hit it, is allowed to catch the ball with the hand or the racket, or to let the ball bounce.

Case 2: During a singles match played on a court with net posts and singles sticks,

the ball served hits a singles stick and then hits the correct service court. Is this a fault?

Decision: Yes.

20. SECOND SERVICE

If the first service is a fault, the server shall serve again without delay from behind the same half of the court from which that fault was served, unless the service was from the wrong half.

21. WHEN TO SERVE & RECEIVE

The server shall not serve until the receiver is ready. However, the receiver shall play to the reasonable pace of the server and shall be ready to receive within a reasonable time of the server being ready.

A receiver who attempts to return the service shall be considered as being ready. If it is demonstrated that the receiver is not ready, the service cannot be called a fault.

22. THE LET DURING A SERVICE

The service is a let if:

a.   The ball served touches the net, strap or band, and is otherwise good; or, after touching the net, strap or band, touches the receiver or the receiver's partner or anything they wear or carry before hitting the ground; or

b.   The ball is served when the receiver is not ready.

In the case of a service let, that particular service shall not count, and the server shall serve again, but a service let does not cancel a previous fault.

Additional approved alternative procedures can be found in Appendix V.

23. THE LET

In all cases when a let is called, except when a service let is called on a second service, the whole point shall be replayed.

Case 1: When the ball is in play, another ball rolls onto court. A let is called. The server had previously served a fault. Is the server now entitled to a first service or second service?

Decision: First service. The whole point must be replayed.

24. PLAYER LOSES
POINT The point is lost
if:

a.   The player serves two consecutive faults; or

b.   The player does not return the ball in play before it bounces twice consecutively; or

c.   The player retu

d.   rns the ball in play so that it hits the ground, or before it bounces, an object, outside the correct court; or

e.   The player returns the ball in play so that, before it bounces, it hits a permanent fixture; or

f.   The receiver returns the service before it bounces; or

g.   The player deliberately carries or catches the ball in play on the racket or deliberately touches it with the racket more than once; or

h.   The player or the racket, whether in the player's hand or not, or anything which the player is wearing or carrying touches the net, net posts/singles sticks, cord or metal cable, strap or band, or the opponent's court at any time while the ball is in play; or

i.   The player hits the ball before it has passed the net; or

j.   The ball in play touches the player or anything that the player is wearing or carrying, except the racket; or

k.   The ball in play touches the racket when the player is not holding it; or

l.   The player deliberately and materially changes the shape of the racket when the ball is in play; or

m.   In doubles, both players touch the ball when returning it.

Case 1: After the server has served a first service, the racket falls out of the server's hand and touches the net before the ball has bounced. Is this a service fault, or does the server lose the point?

Decision: The server loses the point because the racket touches the net while the ball is in play.

Case 2: After the server has served a first service, the racket falls out of the server's hand and touches the net after the ball has bounced outside the correct service court. Is this a service fault, or does the server lose the point?

Decision: This is a service fault because when the racket touched the net the ball was no longer in play.

Case 3: In a doubles match, the receiver's partner touches the net before the ball that has been served touches the ground outside the correct service court. What is the correct decision?

Decision: The receiving team loses the point because the receiver's partner touched the net while the ball was in play.

Case 4: Does a player lose the point if an imaginary line in the extension of the net is crossed before or after hitting the ball?

Decision: The player does not lose the point in either case provided the player does not touch the opponent's court.

Case 5: Is a player allowed to jump over the net into the

opponent's court while the ball is in play?

Decision: No. The player loses the point.

Case 6: A player throws the racket at the ball in play. Both the racket and the ball land in the court on the opponent's side of the net and the opponent(s) is unable to reach the ball. Which player wins the point?

Decision: The player who threw the racket at the ball loses the point.

Case 7: A ball that has just been served hits the receiver or in doubles the receiver's partner before it touches the ground. Which player wins the point? Decision: The server wins the point, unless it is a service let.

Case 8: A player standing outside the court hits the ball or catches it before it bounces and claims the point because the ball was definitely going out of the correct court.

Decision: The player loses the point, unless it is a good return, in which case the point continues.

25. A GOOD
RETURN It is a good return if:

a.   The ball touches the net, net posts/singles sticks, cord or metal cable, strap or band, provided that it passes over any of them and hits the ground within the correct court; except as provided in Rule 2 and 24 (d); or

b.   After the ball in play has hit the ground within the correct court and has spun or been blown back over the net, the player reaches over the net and plays the ball into the correct court, provided that the player does not break Rule 24; or

c.   The ball is returned outside the net posts, either above or below the level of the top of the net, even though it touches the net posts, provided that it hits the ground in the correct court; except as provided in Rules 2 and 24 (d); or

d.   The ball passes under the net cord between the singles stick and the adjacent net post without touching either net, net cord or net post and hits the ground in the correct court, or

e.   The player's racket passes over the net after hitting the ball on the player's own side of the net and the ball hits the ground in the correct court; or

f.   The player hits the ball in play, which hits another ball lying in the correct court.

Case 1: A player returns a ball which then hits a singles stick and hits the ground in the correct court. Is this is a good return?

Decision: Yes. However, if the ball is served and hits the singles stick, it is a service fault.

Case 2: A ball in play hits another ball which is lying in the correct court. What is the correct decision?

Decision: Play continues. However, if it is not clear that the actual ball in play has been returned, a let should be called.

26. HINDRANCE

If a player is hindered in playing the point by a deliberate act of the opponent(s), the player shall win the point.

However, the point shall be replayed if a player is hindered in playing the point by either an unintentional act of the opponent(s), or something outside the player's own control (not including a permanent fixture).

Case 1: Is an unintentional double hit a hindrance?

Decision: No. See also Rule 24 (f).

Case 2: A player claims to have stopped play because the player thought that the opponent(s) was being hindered. Is this a hindrance? Decision: No, the player loses the point.

Case 3: A ball in play hits a bird flying over the court. Is this a hindrance?

Decision: Yes, the point shall be replayed.

Case 4: During a point, a ball or other object that was lying on the player's side of the net when the point started hinders the player. Is this a hindrance? Decision: No.

Case 5: In doubles, where are the server's partner and receiver's partner allowed to stand?

Decision: The server's partner and the receiver's partner may take any position on their own side of the net, inside or outside the court. However, if a player is creating a hindrance to the opponent(s), the hindrance rule should be used.

27. CORRECTING ERRORS

As a principle, when an error in respect of the Rules of Tennis is discovered, all points previously played shall stand. Errors so discovered shall be corrected as follows:

a. During a standard game or a tie-break game, if a player serves from the wrong half of the court, this should be corrected as soon as the error is discovered and the server shall serve from the correct half of the court according to the score. A fault that was served before the error was discovered shall stand.

b. During a standard game or a tie-break game, if the players are at the wrong ends of the court, the error should be corrected as soon as it is discovered and the server shall serve from the correct end of the court according to the score.

c. If a player serves out of turn during a standard game, the player who was originally due to serve shall serve as soon as the error is discovered. However, if a game is completed before the error is discovered the order of service shall remain as altered. In this case, any ball change to be made after an agreed number of games should be made one game later than originally scheduled.

A fault that was served by the opponents(s) before the error was discovered shall not stand.

In doubles, if the partners of one team serve out of turn, a fault that was served before the error was discovered shall stand.

d.   If a player serves out of turn during a tie-break game and the error is discovered after an even number of points have been played, the error is corrected immediately. If the error is discovered after an odd number of points have been played, the order of service shall remain as altered.

A fault that was served by the opponent(s) before the error was discovered shall not stand.

In doubles, if the partners of one team serve out of turn, a fault that was served before the error was discovered shall stand.

e.   During a standard game or a tie-break game in doubles, if there is an error in the order of receiving, this shall remain as altered until the end of the game in which the error is discovered. For the next game in which they are the receivers in that set, the partners shall then resume the original order of receiving.

f.   If in error a tie-break game is started at 6 games all, when it was previously agreed that the set would be an

"Advantage set", the error shall be corrected immediately if only one point has been played. If the error is discovered after the second point is in play, the set will continue as a "Tie-break set".

g.　If in error a standard game is started at 6 games all, when it was previously agreed that the set would be a "Tie-break set", the error shall be corrected immediately if only one point has been played. If the error is discovered after the second point is in play, the set will continue as an "Advantage set" until the score reaches 8 games all (or a higher even number), when a tie-break game shall be played.

h.　If in error an "Advantage set" or "Tie-break set" is started, when it was previously agreed that the final set would be a match tie-break, the error shall be corrected immediately if only one point has been played. If the error is discovered after the second point is in play, the set will continue either until a player or team wins three games (and therefore the set) or until the score reaches 2 games all, when a match tie-break shall be played. However, if the error is discovered after the second point of the fifth game has started, the set will continue as a "Tie-break set". (See Appendix V)

i.　If the balls are not changed in the correct sequence, the error shall be corrected when the player/team who should have served with new balls is next due to serve a new game. Thereafter the balls shall be changed so that the number of games between ball changes shall be that originally agreed. Balls should not be changed during a game.

28. ROLE OF COURT OFFICIALS

For matches where officials are appointed, their roles and responsibilities can be found in Appendix VI.

29. CONTINUOUS PLAY

As a principle, play should be continuous, from the time the match starts (when the first service of the match is put in play) until the match finishes.

a. Between points, a maximum of twenty (20) seconds is allowed. When the players change ends at the end of a game, a maximum of ninety (90) seconds are allowed. However, after the first game of each set and during a tie-break game, play shall be continuous and the players shall change ends without a rest.

   At the end of each set there shall be a set break of a maximum of one hundred and twenty (120) seconds.

   The maximum time starts from the moment that one point finishes until the first service is struck for the next point.

   Event organisers may apply for ITF approval to extend the ninety (90) seconds allowed when the players change ends at the end of a game and the one hundred and twenty (120) seconds allowed at a set break.

b. If, for reasons outside the player's control, clothing, footwear or necessary equipment (excluding the racket) is broken or needs to be replaced, the player may be allowed reasonable extra time to rectify the problem.

c. No extra time shall be given to allow a player to recover condition. However, a player suffering from a treatable medical condition may be allowed one medical time-out of three minutes for the treatment of that medical condition. A limited number of toilet/change of attire breaks may also be allowed, if this is announced in advance of the event.

d.   Event organisers may allow a rest period of a maximum of ten (10) minutes if this is announced in advance of the event. This rest period can be taken after the 3rd set in a best of 5 sets match, or after the 2nd set in a best of 3 sets match.

e.   The warm-up time shall be a maximum of five (5) minutes, unless otherwise decided by the event organisers.

30. COACHING

Coaching is considered to be communication, advice or instruction of any kind and by any means to a player.

In team events where there is a team captain sitting on-court, the team captain may coach the player(s) during a set break and when the players change ends at the end of a game, but not when the players change ends after the first game of each set and not during a tie-break game.

In all other matches, coaching is not allowed.

Case 1: Is a player allowed to be coached, if the coaching is given by signals in a discreet way?

Decision: No.

Case 2: Is a player allowed to receive coaching when play is suspended?

Decision: Yes.

Case 3: Is a player allowed to receive on-court coaching during a match?

Decision: Sanctioning bodies may apply to the ITF to have on-court coaching allowed. In events where on-court coaching is allowed, designated coaches may enter the court and coach their players under procedures decided by the sanctioning body.

APPENDIX. II. GLOSSARY OF TENNIS TERMS

A

• Ace: a service point won by the server because the receiver doesn't return, or even touch, the ball.

• Advantage (or ad) court: left-hand side of the court.

• Advantage (or Ad): the point played after deuce, which if won, ends the game.

• Advantage set: a set that can only be won when one opponent has won six games and is two games clear of their opponent. The final sets of singles matches at the Australian Open, French Open, Wimbledon, Davis Cup and the Olympics are all advantage sets.

• All: term used when both players have the same number of points from 15-15 (15-all) to 30-30 (30-all). When the score is 40-40 the term is deuce.

• All-court player: someone who is equally comfortable playing from the baseline, mid-court and net.

• Alley: (see tramlines.)

• Approach shot: a shot used by a player to pin their opponent behind the baseline so that they can run to the net for a volley.

• ATP: Association of Tennis Professionals, the governing body of men's tennis.

• ATP World Tour: circuit of men's professional tennis tournaments.

• Australian Open: First Grand Slam tournament of the tennis calendar played in January at Melbourne Park on blue Plexicushion courts.

B

• Back court: area behind the court between the baseline and the back fence.

• Backhand: shot struck by holding the racquet in the dominant hand but swinging the racquet from the non-dominant side of the body with the back of the dominant hand pointing in the direction the ball is being hit. (See also two-handed backhand.)

• Backspin: spin imparted on the underside of the ball causing it to revolve backwards while travelling forwards. Used in slice and drop shots.

• Backswing: component of the swing where the racquet is taken back behind the body in preparation for the forward motion that leads to contact with the ball.

• Bagel: colloquial term for winning or losing a set to love, the 0 in the score line evoking the shape of a bagel.

• Ballkid: boy or girl (or man or woman) responsible for retrieving tennis balls that are out of play and supplying them to the server before each point.

• Baseline: the line at each end of the court behind which the server stands to serve.

• Baseliner: a player who prefers to play at the baseline, relying on their groundstrokes.

• Break: a service game that is won by the player receiving serve.

• Break back: game won by a receiver who has previously conceded their own service game during the same set.

• Break point: point held by a receiver that, if won, earns them their opponent's service game. The scores 0-40, 15-40, 30-40 and 40-Ad are all break points.

• Bye: situation in which a player advances automatically to the next round of a tournament without having to play a match. Generally a privilege extended to seeded players in the opening round of a tournament.

C

• Call: a player or court official's decision as to whether a ball was in or out.

• Chalk: the material used to mark court lines on grass courts.

• Challenge: disputing what a player believes to be an incorrect line call via video line-calling.

• Challenger tournaments: week-long ITF events positioned one tier below ATP and WTA Tour tournaments that are staged all over the world and are part of the Pro Tour in Australia.

• Champions' tiebreak: method used to decide the outcome of a doubles match, usually when players are at one set-all. Players alternate serve with the first to reach 10 points with a two-point advantage winning the match.

• Change of ends: ninety-second rest period taken courtside, between odd games, before players move to the other end of the court and continue play.

• Chip: Method of using underpin to block a shot back into court. Sometimes used as a tactic to counteract a powerful serve.

• Chip-and-charge: tactic whereby a player chips the ball into their opponent's court and immediately approaches the net for a volley.

• Clay court: playing surface made of finely powdered red or green clay.

• Code violation: penalty for breaking tennis' code of conduct rules. The first infraction incurs a warning, the second a point penalty, the third a game penalty and the fourth results in default from the match.

• Counterpuncher: player who employs a defensive playing style.

• Court: the area within which a match is played.

• Cross-court shot: shot hit from one corner of the court to the diagonally opposite corner.

• Cyclops: device used prior to video line-calling to determine whether a serve was in or out.

D

• Davis Cup: annual international men's team competition staged by the ITF.

• Dead rubber: match played after the result of a team competition has already been decided. In men's tennis the number of sets played is usually reduced from best of five to three, or teams may agree not to play dead rubbers.

• Deep: a shot that lands near the baseline rather than mid-court, generally putting the player who receives it under pressure.

• Default: disqualification of a player due to code violations.

• Deuce: terminology for the score when it stands at 40-40. A player must win two-consecutive points from deuce in order to win the game.

• Deuce court: the right-hand side of the court.

• Dink: shot hit with little power or pace that just clears the net.

• Dirt-baller: colloquial term for a claycourt specialist.

• Double fault: consecutive faults on serve, resulting in the returner winning the point.

• Doubles: a match between teams of two players.

• Down the line: shot hit straight down the court, close to one of the sidelines.

• Drop shot: a delicate shot employing backspin that drops just over the net.

Drop volley: a delicate volley employing touch that drops just over the net.

E

• En Tout Cas: playing surface made from coarse crushed red brick material.

• Error: a shot that lands out, or doesn't clear the net, resulting in the loss of a point.

• Exhibition: match or tournament played for entertainment and prize money but not for ranking points.

F

• Fault: a serve that hits the net or doesn't land within the service box and consequently does not start the point. Consecutive faults are termed a double fault and result in the loss of a point.

• Fed Cup: annual international women's team competition staged by the ITF.

• Fifteen: opening point of a game for either player or team.

• First serve: the first of two serves a player is allowed in order to start a point.

• Follow through: component of the swing after the racquet has connected with the ball.

• Foot fault: penalty when a serving player steps on or over the baseline, or over the baseline's centre mark, before connecting with the ball, resulting in a service fault.

• Forced error: an error made off a difficult shot hit by an opponent.

• Forehand: stroke made with the front of the dominant hand facing the direction in which the ball is being struck.

• Forty: the third point won in a game by either player or team. If both parties reach 40 it is called deuce.

• French Open: second Grand Slam of the tournament calendar. Played on clay courts in May at Roland Garros in Paris.

• Futures: week-long ITF men's events positioned one tier below ATP Tour tournaments that are staged all over the world and are part of the Pro Tour in Australia.

G

• GOAT: acronym for Greatest Of All Time.

• Game: the building blocks of a set. Each set must comprise at least six games.

• Game point: a point that, if won, will result in a player winning the game they are playing.

• Game, set, match: the words a match umpire uses to indicate that a match has concluded.

• Golden Grand Slam: the feat whereby a player wins all four Grand Slam tournaments and an Olympic gold medal in the same year.

• Grand Slam: the feat whereby a player wins all four Grand Slam tournaments in the same year. Also know as majors, the four Grand Slam tournaments are the most prestigious tennis tournaments on the annual calendar, offering the most ranking points and the highest amount of prize money. The Grand Slams are the Australian Open, the French Open, Wimbledon and the US Open.

• Groundstroke: shots hit from on, or behind, the baseline after the ball has bounced.

• Grunting: noise emitted by players through exertion or as a breathing technique as they are hitting the ball.

H

• Hacker: player with an unconventional or un-coached playing style.

• Half volley: volley made off a low-bouncing ball by placing the racquet close to the court surface.

• Hawk-Eye: system of video line-calling employed by the Grand Slams.

• Hold serve: situation in which a serving player wins their service game.

• Hot Dog: trick shot whereby a player chases down a lob, then hits the ball between his legs from behind the baseline with his back to the net.

I

• formation: doubles formation where the net player on the serving team straddles the centre service line at a crouch with the aim of cutting off a cross-court return.

• In: call made when a ball falls within the playing area.

• ITF: International Tennis Federation, the world governing body of tennis.

K

• Kick serve: a serve where the ball is imparted with topspin making it "kick" up upon connecting with the court surface.

L

• Let: a stroke or point that doesn't count and has to be replayed. Occurs when a serve clips the net before bouncing into the service box, when a point is interrupted by outside interference or if an umpire overrules a call made by a linesperson.

• Linesperson (line judge): court official responsible for making calls on a particular line.

• Lob: high-arcing shot intended to pass over an opponent's head and land within the playing area.

• Long: alternative call to "out" when a ball lands beyond the baseline.

• Love: tennis word for zero, meaning no points in a game or a set.

• Love game: a game won by a player without their opponent scoring any points.

• Lucky loser: player who loses in qualifying but gets into the main draw of a tournament due to another player withdrawing. A lucky loser berth is generally awarded to the highest ranked non-qualifying player.

M

• Match: competitive format for tennis usually decided by the best of three or the best of five sets.

• Match point: point in a match that, if won, brings the match to an end.

• Mini-break: a tiebreak point won on an opponent's serve.

• Miss-hit: shot struck with the ball not connecting fully with the strings.

• Mixed doubles: doubles match played with one male and one female opponent on team.

• Moonball: stroke played with heavy topspin to slow down a point or help a player to recover their position on court.

N

• Net: netting stretched horizontally across the mid-point of the court, supported by net posts, that measures 91.5 cm at the centre strap and 106.5 cm at the net posts.

• Net chord: white band from which the length of the net is suspended.

• Net point: point decided at the net, usually by a volley (as opposed to a point won or lost at the baseline).

• New balls: in a match, a new set of balls replaces those in play initially after the first seven games, and then every nine games thereafter.

• No-man's land: the area between the baseline and service line where it is difficult for players to make effective shots.

O

• Official: member of the on-court officiating team. Includes the umpire, linespeople, court supervisor and referee.

• Out: call made when a ball lands outside the playing area.

• Overhead: see smash.

• Overrule: decision made by an umpire to reverse a call made by a linesperson.

P

• Passing shot: shot that passes to the left or right of a net player (not over them) and lands within the playing area.

• Plexicushion: hardcourt surface used at Australian Open Series events.

• Poach: doubles maneuver whereby a net player intercepts a shot directed at their partner.

• Protected ranking: special ranking given to a player returning from an injury break of more than six months, based on their average ranking during the first three months of injury, used to help them gain direct entry into tournament main draws or qualifying to assist their comeback.

• Pusher: term used to refer to a player whose game is based on keeping the ball in play rather than aggressively trying to hit winners.

Q

• Qualifying (Qualies): preliminary event that offers players whose rankings don't gain them direct entry in the main draw of a tournament, the opportunity to win a spot in that main draw.

• Qualifier: person that wins through to the main draw of a tournament via qualifying.

R

• Racquet (Racket): piece of equipment with a long handle and strung oval head used to hit the ball during a tennis match.

• Rally: exchange of a series of tennis strokes during a game that ends when a player makes an error or hits a shot that their opponent can't return.

• Receiver: player returning serve.

• Referee: senior official responsible for enforcing tournament rules.

• Reflex volley: instinctive volley made with no time to think about the shot or get the racquet in position.

• Retirement: withdrawal of a player during a match, usually due to injury and illness.

• Round robin: style of tournament play whereby the draw is divided into similar sized groups and each player has to play every other player within their group.

Rubber: an alternative word to "match" used in team tennis play.

S

• Second serve: literally the second of two serves a player is allowed per point (discounting let serves) which, if missed, results in a double fault and the point being conceded.

• Seed: highly ranked player whose position in a tournament

draw has been arranged so that they do not meet another highly-ranked player until the latter stages of the tournament.

• Serve: over-arm stroke played from behind the baseline and to one side of the centre mark, used to start a point.

• Serve and volley: style of play whereby a player serves the ball and then rushes the net in order to finish the point early with a volley.

• Set point: point that, if won by the player who holds it, brings a set to an end.

• Shank: miss-hit stroke resulting in a misdirected shot.

• Singles: tennis game played by two opponents.

• Singles sticks: poles, positioned on the singles sidelines, used to support the net during singles play.

• Sitter: mid-court ball that is easy to put away.

• Slice: net-skimming shot hit with under spin and sidespin.

• Smash: stroke similar to a service action played when the ball is travelling above a player's head, for example off a lob.

• Spin: direction in which the surface of a ball rotates while travelling through the air (includes topspin, underspin, sidespin).

• Split step: checking step made by incoming volleyers to adjust their footwork as they gauge the path of an oncoming ball.

• Straight sets: a match won without the loss of a set.

• Strings: synthetic or gut material from which the playing

surface of a tennis racquet is woven.

• String savers: small pieces of plastic inserted where strings cross to prevent wear and string breakages.

• Stroke: way in which a tennis ball is struck.

• Sudden death: point that, if won, brings a game or tiebreak to an end without the need for a player to be two points clear of their opponent.

• Sweet spot: point on the racquet strings at which the ball rebounds optimally.

T

• Tanking: colloquial term for losing a game, set or match on purpose.

• Tape: white synthetic material used to mark the lines on clay and En Tout Cas courts. (Alternatively see net chord.)

• Tennis ball: pressurised, air-filled rubber ball covered externally by felt, struck by a racquet in the sport of tennis.

• Tennis elbow: common tennis injury in which the muscles and tendons of the elbow and forearm become inflamed and painful.

• Thirty: second point in a game for either player or team.

• Tie: collective term referring to the group of matches or rubbers played between two teams in a team tennis event.

• Tiebreak: method used to decide the outcome of a set,

usually when players are at six games-all. Players alternate serve with the first to reach seven points with a two point advantage winning the set. (See also Champions tiebreak.)

• Topspin: spin imparted on a tennis ball by stroking it from low to high, causing it to rotate forwards as it moves through the air and bounce high upon landing.

• Touch: descriptive term that refers to a player's ability to maneuver a ball delicately.

• Tramlines: external court lines that run parallel to the singles lines, defining the area of play for doubles.

• Two-handed backhand: backhand stroke where the racquet handle is also supported by the non-dominant hand.

U

• Underspin: spin imparted on a ball that causes it rotate backwards as it travels forwards.

• Umpire: court official responsible for monitoring the calls made by linespeople and enforcing the rules of tennis during a match.

• Underarm serve: alternative (and rarely-used) service technique that sees the server deliver the ball underarm rather than by the traditional over-arm method.

• Unforced error: error committed due to poor technique or judgment on a player's part rather than as the result of a good shot by their opponent.

• US Open: fourth and final Grand Slam tournament of the

calendar year, played at Flushing Meadows in New York.

• Unseeded: term given to a player whose ranking does not afford them a protected (seeded) position in the draw.

V

• Video line-calling: digital system for making line calls that uses video cameras and action replays to determine whether balls are in or out.

• Volley: forehand or backhand stroke executed at the net before the ball bounces, the racquet moving in a punching motion.

W

• Walkover: victory awarded to a player when their opponent concedes a match before it begins, usually due to injury or illness.

• Wide: call made when a ball lands outside the singles or doubles playing area.

• Wildcard: free pass into a tournament draw awarded when a player's ranking is not high enough to gain them direct entry or they have not entered the tournament by the closing date for entries.

• Wimbledon: third Grand Slam tournament of the tennis calendar, also known as The Championships. Played on grass at the All England Lawn Tennis and Croquet Club in South West London.

• Winner: shot that lands within the playing area and ends a point because the person receiving it is unable to return it effectively.

• WTA Tour: Women's Tennis Association Tour, the governing body of the women's game

ABOUT THE AUTHOR

.Sports maniac
.Math teacher, Engineer
.Travel writer
.Born in Korea
.Lived in China, Canada and so on.
.Living in Slovakia, Europe.
.Believing in the power of positive thinking

"Stay hungry. Stay foolish." -Steve Jobs

Printed in Great Britain
by Amazon

27149722R00067